Living Standards in the United States

Living Standards in the United States

A Consumption-Based Approach

Daniel T. Slesnick

The AEI Press

Publisher for the American Enterprise Institute

WASHINGTON, D.C.

2000

Available in the United States from AEI Press, c/o Publisher Resources Inc., 1224 Heil Quaker Blvd., P.O. Box 7001, La Vergne, TN 37086-7001. Distributed outside the United States by arrangement with Eurospan, 3 Henrietta Street, London WC2E 8LU England.

ISBN 0-8447-7142-2

1 3 5 7 9 10 8 6 4 2

THE AEI PRESS
Publisher for the American Enterprise Institute
1150 Seventeenth Street, N.W.
Washington, D.C. 20036

Printed in the United States of America

Contents

Foreword

This study is one of a series commissioned by the American Enterprise Institute on trends in the level and distribution of U.S. wages, income, wealth, consumption, and other measures of material welfare. The issues addressed in the series involve much more than dry statistics: they touch on fundamental aspirations of the American people—material progress, widely shared prosperity, and just reward for individual effort—and affect popular understanding of the successes and shortcomings of the private market economy and of particular government policies. For these reasons, discussions of "economic inequality" in the media and political debate are often partial and partisan as well as superficial. The AEI series is intended to improve the public discussion by bringing new data to light, exploring the strengths and weaknesses of various measures of economic welfare, and highlighting important questions of interpretation, causation, and consequence.

Each study in the series is presented and discussed in draft form at an AEI seminar before publication by the AEI Press. Marvin Kosters, director of economic policy studies at AEI, organized the series and moderated the seminars. A current list of published studies appears on the last page.

CHRISTOPHER C. DEMUTH
President
American Enterprise Institute
for Public Policy Research

Acknowledgments

I would like to thank Dale Jorgenson, Marvin Kosters, and John Weicher, among many others, for helpful comments and discussions on the issues presented in this study. A fuller exposition of the results presented here can be found in my forthcoming book, *Consumption and Social Welfare*.

Introduction

Over the course of virtually every national presidential election we are asked whether we are better off than we were four years ago. The question is almost always rhetorical; the "correct" answer depends on one's political persuasion and on who's in the White House. Many economists have attempted to address the standard-of-living issue objectively and, for the most part, their findings paint a bleak picture. Real median family income has changed little since the early 1970s, which has led some analysts to conclude that, for the first time since the Great Depression, the younger generations are at risk of having lower standards of living than their parents.

Not only is the size of the pie fixed, but it is being more unequally distributed as well. Much has been made of the infamous U-turn in income inequality. The Bureau of the Census has reported that family income inequality decreased through the late 1960s and then, by 1998, increased to its highest level since World War II. Such statistics cannot help but prompt concern about economic polarization in the United States.

The official poverty statistics have added fuel to the fire. The poverty rate exhibited a trend that was approximately the mirror image of median family income: it fell through the early 1970s and then increased in the 1980s. In 1993, 15.1 percent of the population was below the poverty line, a level that exceeded the poverty rate in 1966. The unhappy conclusion is that the gains in alleviating poverty in the first half of the postwar era were followed by a conspicuous lack of progress, despite a concerted and expensive government initiative that began with President Johnson's War on Poverty.

The evidence I shall present shows that this pessimistic view of social welfare in the United States is unwarranted. The erroneous conclusions arise from several features of the method used by the Bureau of the Census and others to measure welfare. While economic well-being is almost always measured using family income, a more accurate assessment of the standard of living is based on what families consume. That provides a better "snapshot" of how the family is doing, and more accurately approximates lifetime well-being as well. Failure to account for heterogeneity across families (such as differences in size) is another important source of error. Consumption-based social welfare statistics that adjust for differences in family size show that the standard of living has been rising rather than stagnating. Consumption-based inequality estimates that account for heterogeneity across households are lower than the Census Bureau's estimates and exhibit a markedly different trend. Poverty rates based on the consumption levels of households are also dramatically lower than the official statistics tabulated using families' incomes.

Conceptual Issues

How should well-being be measured? Welfare measurement is a fundamental element of economic analysis, but undertaking the measurement is an activity fraught with peril. Well-being is influenced by a number of factors related not only to individuals' economic position but also to their social, political, physical, emotional, and psychological status. The definition of welfare most commonly used by policy analysts focuses exclusively on material well-being. Measuring an inherently multidimensional concept by a single statistic almost certainly ignores relevant information. One could easily argue that living standards should be evaluated using information other than economic status. Rather than tackle that daunting task, I acknowledge at the outset that I am looking at only one of many aspects of the standard of living.[1]

Choosing an "Income" Variable. Given this restricted focus, the first, and perhaps most important, choice is the "income" variable to be used to measure material well-being.[2] Under ideal circumstances, welfare would be estimated on the basis of the income received over the individual's lifetime. But that is generally infeasible because it depends on variables that are inherently unobservable. There are no data in the United States, for example, that follow individuals over their entire lives, and inferences drawn from observable variables can be misleading. As a result, most empirical studies measure welfare over a shorter time horizon, such as a year.

As a snapshot of the standard of living, economic theory unambiguously recommends that consumption, rather than income, be used to assess economic well-being. The ultimate satisfaction of the individual is derived from the goods and services consumed. Consumption can differ from income because of the ability of consumers to borrow and save, and because some goods are received without explicit payments, such as in-kind transfers and public goods.

As an added advantage, consumption provides a more accurate approximation of lifetime or permanent income. The two leading theories of consumption behavior suggest that spending decisions are made on the basis of expected lifetime income rather than on the basis of the income received in a single year.[3] As income fluctuates from year to year, individuals smooth their consumption by saving and dissaving in order to maintain their standard of living. Under those circumstances, consumption serves as a more accurate proxy for welfare (relative to income) over a longer time horizon.

This alternative approach to welfare measurement

obviously requires an explicit definition of consumption. Spending on nondurable goods and services is an important component and is easily estimated, but the consumption of other items is not as straightforward to measure. It is inappropriate, for example, to classify durable purchases as consumption, because that would imply a high level of consumption in the years in which a purchase is made, and zero consumption in other years. In fact, services are received over the useful life of durable goods, and the definition of consumption should reflect that feature. The same type of argument can be made for owner-occupied housing.

Some items are consumed (and affect the standard of living) without observable transactions. In-kind transfers such as food stamps, housing subsidies, and Medicaid are provided to poor households at little or no cost to recipients. Public goods increase the overall standard of living but can have different effects on welfare levels depending on how they are valued. Police protection, for example, is important to somebody living in a high crime area but is, perhaps, of less concern to an individual who lives in a safe neighborhood.

As with durable services, in-kind transfers, and public goods, the quantity of leisure consumed is difficult to observe because it involves no explicit market transaction. But it undoubtedly affects both the level and distribution of well-being. Two individuals who consume the same quantities of goods and services but have vastly different amounts of free time are not equally well-off. The rise in labor-force participation by women suggests that leisure plays an increasingly important role in the measurement of the standard of living in the United States. One could argue that median family income (or any other similar index) overstates the level and trend of social welfare because it is now produced by multiple earners. Real incomes are the same, but the amount of leisure consumed (and the standard of living) has actually fallen.[4]

Measuring the Cost of Living. Whether income or expenditures are used to measure the standard of living, intertemporal comparisons require that nominal variables be deflated by a price index to account for changes in prices. Over the years, the consumer price index (CPI) has been used extensively, and virtually exclusively, as the government's estimate of the cost of living, despite increasing evidence of systematic biases.[5]

In most applications of cost-of-living indexes, the central issue is the amount by which nominal wages, benefits, or expenditures need to change to maintain a constant level of well-being. The CPI is ill-suited for calculating that figure, and, in recent years, the magnitudes of the biases have been large. Part of the bias can be attributed to the fact that the weights used to calculate the index are assumed to be fixed over time, while household-expenditure patterns shift.[6] Another problem is in the treatment of owner-occupied housing. Prior to 1983, the weight representing the budget share of owner-occupied housing was calculated using the investment expenditures of homeowners (the spending on taxes, insurance, and mortgage interest) rather than the flow of services or rental equivalent of the home. The high interest rates in the 1970s resulted in an overestimate of the increase in the price of housing, and the CPI was too high. The effect of this error was that inflation was overstated, and, in some years, the magnitude of the bias was large.[7] While the treatment of housing in the CPI was modified after 1983, there was no historical revision of the index. The post-1983 CPI is, therefore, inconsistent with the estimates of the price level before 1983.[8]

To assess the degree to which the CPI mismeasures inflation, I compare it with two alternative indexes. The first is an experimental index produced by the Bureau of Labor Statistics (BLS) that treats owner-occupied housing consistently throughout the sample period.[9] Any difference between that index and the CPI is the result of the inappropriate treatment of owner-occupied housing in the CPI. The second index is cal-culated using the implicit price deflators of personal consumption expenditures (PCE). The fixed-weight assumption is relaxed, and owner-occupied housing is treated appropriately as the rental equivalent of the home throughout the sample period.[10]

The estimated inflation rates for the three indexes are shown in figure 1. Each series exhibits the same qualitative pattern of price movements since World War II. Prices fluctuated sharply until the early 1960s, when inflation began to rise. Price increases accelerated in the 1970s, fueled partly by the oil-price shocks of 1973–

FIGURE 1
ANNUAL INFLATION RATES, 1948–1995

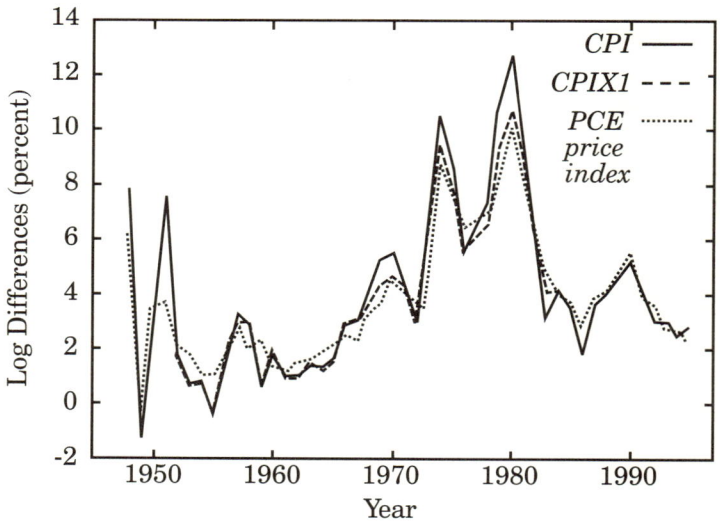

SOURCE: CPI and CPIX1 are obtained from the Bureau of Labor Statistics. The PCE price index is calculated in the manner de-scribed in note 10, using the implicit price deflators of personal con-sumption expenditures in the National Income and Product Accounts.

1974 and 1979–1980. Each index shows a significant decrease in inflation after 1980. Over the entire period, the CPI-based estimate of the average inflation rate was 4.0 percent per year compared with the 3.8 percent obtained using the other two indexes.

While the same qualitative pattern of price movements is found for each price index, in some years the differences are very large. Over the fifteen-year period between 1967 and 1982, the housing bias caused the CPI and CPIX1 to diverge. Between 1977 and 1982 the CPI recorded an average inflation rate of 9.3 percent per year, compared with 8.3 percent for the CPIX1 and 8.1 percent for the PCE price index. Between 1979 and 1980 the CPI rose 12.7 percent, while the inflation rate measured by the CPIX1 was 10.6 percent.

What are the implications of these results? The CPI's overestimate of inflation in the 1970s and 1980s resulted in permanent overinflation of the poverty thresholds, and poverty rates were biased upward. Standard-of-living indexes that used the CPI to deflate nominal income or expenditures were biased downward, and growth rates in the 1970s and 1980s were underestimated. Perhaps most important, all of the government's transfers and benefits that were indexed to the CPI over this period were overinflated, which increased the deficit and resulted in the overpayment of billions of dollars.[11]

Comparing Household Welfare. Perhaps the most controversial aspect of welfare measurement is comparison of the well-being of heterogeneous households. If a two-adult household has the same expenditure as another composed of two adults and two children, what can be said of their relative welfare levels? An answer to that simple question is fundamentally important to the evaluation of the standard of living and to measuring inequality and poverty.

One could make arguments that span the spectrum of possibilities. We are all familiar with the old adage that two can live as cheaply as one. If that observation is taken literally, the two households in the preceding paragraph are viewed as equally well-off. Perhaps a more plausible argument is that the households' "needs" are different but that their welfare is not. If fertility is perfectly controllable and family size is a choice rather than a constraint, the increase in well-being associated with a larger family exactly compensates for the increase in consumption requirements. That assumption is implicit in the use of real median family income as a measure of social welfare and the Gini coefficient of family income as a measure of inequality.

This method of comparing welfare levels fails to account for the fact that fertility decisions are made over the course of a lifetime in an environment of uncertainty. One's ex ante assessment of welfare may not coincide with ex post reality, and unlike other goods, children cannot be discarded to obtain the "optimal" consumption bundle. Furthermore, there is the presumption that only the parents' preferences matter. The parents may be equally well-off with the arrival of an additional child, but what of the other children, who must share a fixed level of resources with more people?[12]

At the opposite end of the spectrum is the idea that households' needs increase linearly and identically with each additional member. That assumption is implicit in the use of per capita income, which implies that a household with two adults and two children attains a standard of living equal to one-half that of two adults with the same income. While that measure is frequently used, it relies on the dubious assumption that the needs of a child are the same as those of an adult. Another implication is that there are no economies of scale in consumption. While doubling the number of family members *may* double the food requirements, it is unlikely that the larger family needs twice the spending on housing, televisions, or utilities.

If one rejects these two methods of accounting for heterogeneity, how should one compare the needs of different households? A more sophisticated method of head-counting involves estimating the number of "equivalent adults" in the household. If, for example, children are equivalent to half an adult in terms of their needs, a couple with two children would form a household with three adult equivalents and have 50 percent greater consumption requirements than a childless couple with the same expenditure—and enjoy two-thirds the welfare. With economies of scale in consumption, the number of equivalent adults would be even lower.

The number of equivalent adults in households has been estimated in a variety of ways.[13] For the purpose of measuring the poverty rate, the Bureau of the Census uses an estimate of need that is based on the nutritional requirements of different types of families.[14] Other estimates are based on experts' opinions of households' consumption requirements. While objective empirical evidence undoubtedly influences those opinions, they are also influenced by political and legal considerations. A third approach estimates household equivalence scales using information on households' spending patterns on goods and services. Given the variety of methods, the absence of consensus as to the right way to account for differences in needs is not surprising. Accordingly, I present estimates of the standard of living and its distribution using different sets of equivalence scales.

The measure of welfare used in subsequent empirical work can be represented as follows:

$$W_k = \frac{M_k}{P_k \, N_k} \tag{1}$$

where M_k is total expenditure (the nominal value of consumption), P_k is a household-specific price index, and N_k is the number of equivalent adults in the household. The numerator in equation (1), total expenditure, is the nominal value of our measure of economic well-being. The price index, P_k, is used to adjust the welfare measure for inflation and to facilitate comparisons over time. The equivalence scale takes into account that families or households are heterogeneous and have different consumption requirements. Per capita measures, for example, take N_k to be the number of persons in the household.

How does this index differ from real family income, the measure often used by policy analysts to evaluate the standard of living? The "income" concept is consumption rather than before-tax income, which, in and of itself, yields dramatically different conclusions concerning both levels and trends of living standards in the United States. While measures of welfare based on family income ignore heterogeneity, the consumption-based index (equation [1]) accounts for differences in preferences through the equivalence scales. The differential impacts of relative price changes on households are accounted for through the price indexes P_k. The cost of living varies across households to the extent that their expenditure patterns are different. An increase in the price of necessities, for example, hurts poor households more than rich ones.

The Standard of Living

While the measurement of welfare at the micro level is an essential first step, analysts are primarily concerned with the impacts of policies on groups of households. Changes in public policy result in both winners and losers so that, for welfare economics to be useful to practitioners, a method of aggregating these effects is essential. This requires normative judgments in which the benefits to some are balanced against the losses to others.[15]

I define a consumption-based standard of living index as a needs-adjusted measure of aggregate consumption:

$$W = \frac{\Sigma M_k}{P \; \Sigma N_k}. \tag{2}$$

The numerator is the level of spending by all households, P is a national price index, and ΣN_k is an estimate of the total number of equivalent adults in the population, which is intended to measure the aggregate consumption requirements of the population. Note that equation (2) is independent of the distribution, because a transfer of resources from a rich household to a poor household leaves W unchanged. I choose this particular index not because distributional considerations are viewed as unimportant, but to maintain comparability with commonly used income-based measures of social welfare.[16]

Many of the standard-of-living indexes used by analysts are special cases of equation (2). Real per capita income, for example, replaces total expenditure with income, uses the CPI as a price deflator, and measures the aggregate consumption requirements using the number of persons. Real family income is the same, except that aggregate need is represented by the number of families. Real GDP, which is sometimes used as an estimate of social welfare, replaces aggregate expenditure with GDP and makes no adjustment for the consumption requirements of families or households.

Consumption-based indexes of the standard of living reveal a more optimistic picture of the growth of living standards in the United States than do income-based indexes. In figure 2, I present estimates of per capita consumption over the period from 1947 through 1995.[17] This is the simplest form of the index defined in equation (2), with aggregate need measured by the total population. While this indicator of the standard of liv-

FIGURE 2
CONSUMPTION-BASED STANDARD OF LIVING, 1947–1995

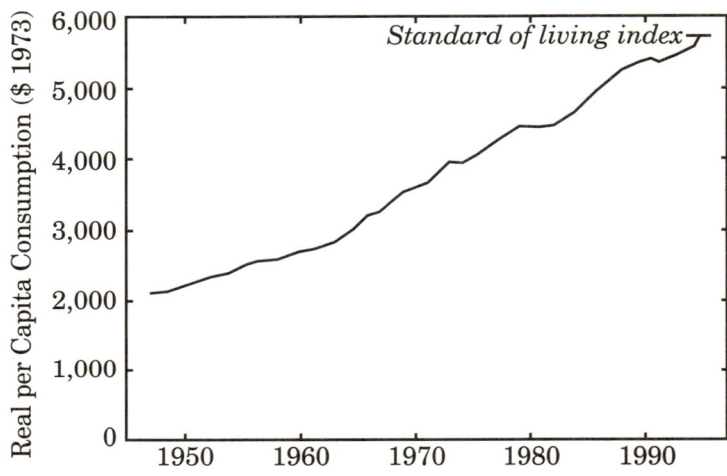

SOURCE: Author's calculations using the PCE (modified in the manner described in note 17), the PCE price index, and population estimates from the Bureau of the Census.

ing has many shortcomings, I present it initially because it is most easily compared with widely reported income statistics.

What is most evident from figure 2 is that the standard of living increased steadily after 1947; the average growth rate over the entire period was 2.1 percent per year. Far from being stagnant recently, it increased at an average rate of 1.9 percent per year after 1971. The average growth rates across decades were uneven: 2.0 percent per year in the 1950s, 2.9 percent in the 1960s, 2.2 percent in the 1970s, 1.9 percent in the 1980s, and 1.3 percent in the first half of the 1990s.

That picture of living standards is in marked contrast with what is indicated by real median family income, shown in figure 3. Over the forty-eight years, the average increase for median family income (adjusted for

FIGURE 3
AVERAGE STANDARD OF LIVING, 1947–1995

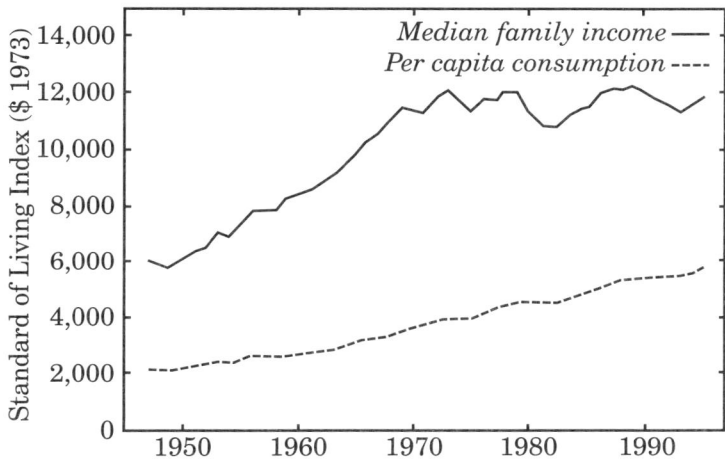

SOURCE: Per capita consumption is calculated as in figure 2. Median family income is obtained from the Bureau of the Census and is deflated using the CPI.

inflation) was only 1.4 percent per year, with virtually all the growth occurring before 1971. The absence of growth in this index after the early 1970s prompted dire predictions of a decline in the standard of living of future generations. The consumption-based estimates are clearly at odds with this conclusion; there is no indication that living standards are in jeopardy in the United States.

What might account for the inaccuracy of real median family income as a measure of the average standard of living? First and foremost, the income of the median family need not be representative of the entire population. It is easy to come up with examples in which median income provides a distorted picture of living standards. If, for example, the incomes of families below the median decrease, and every other family is unaffected, the median is unchanged—even though most would agree that, on average, the standard of living fell.

Using the family as the basic observational unit also ignores the fact that its composition has changed over time. Because average family size has decreased, the consumption requirements per family have also decreased, and median family income understates the trend in the standard of living. Note, also, that restricting the focus to families ignores what the Bureau of the Census calls "unrelated individuals." Unrelated individuals have become an increasingly important segment of the population, and omitting them from the sample could have a significant effect on estimates of the standard of living and its distribution.[18]

Median family income in figure 3 is adjusted for inflation using the CPI. It was shown in figure 1 that CPI-based inflation estimates were biased upward and the magnitudes of the biases were particularly large in the late 1970s and early 1980s. CPI-deflated indexes, therefore, underestimate the growth rate of the standard of living over this period. A final (and perhaps most important) source of divergence between median family income and per capita consumption arises from the use of income as a measure of material well-being rather than consumption.

What is the relative importance of each of these factors? Table 1 shows that median family income and per capita consumption diverged over the second half of the sample period; per capita consumption grew at an average rate of 1.9 percent per year, compared with 0.2 percent for median family income. The fraction of this difference that can be attributed to the bias in the CPI can be determined by comparing the growth rates of per capita consumption using, separately, the PCE price index and the CPI as deflators. As expected, the index calculated using the CPI shows less growth but cannot explain much of the difference between median family

TABLE 1
AVERAGE ANNUAL GROWTH RATES, 1947–1995
(percent)

	Total	1947–1970	1971–1995
Per Capita Consumption (PCE deflator)	2.10	2.31	1.89
Per Capita Consumption (CPI deflator)	1.96	2.21	1.71
Per Capita Income (CPI deflator)	1.86	2.51	1.22
Real Median Family Income (CPI deflator)	1.40	2.60	0.20

SOURCE: Author's calculations using the PCE, *Current Population Reports, Series P-60,* and the CPI.

income and per capita consumption. Between 1971 and 1995 the CPI-adjusted estimates of per capita consumption grew at an average rate of 1.7 percent per year; the CPI bias explains only 11 percent of the difference in growth rates.

Per capita income grew 1.2 percent per year between 1971 and 1995; the substitution of income for consumption therefore accounts for roughly 29 percent of the difference in growth rates. The remainder of the gap (60 percent) arises from the failure to account for changes in average family size and the omission of unrelated individuals from the tabulations.[19] This gap also reflects differences that result from using the median as a summary statistic rather than using a sample average.

The overall conclusion is that reports of stagnant or decreasing levels of social welfare are inaccurate. Between 1947 and 1995, per capita consumption increased at an average rate of 2.1 percent per year. The highest growth rate occurred in the 1960s, but even as recently as the 1980s the standard of living as measured by per capita consumption grew at a rate approximately equal to the postwar average. This qualitative conclusion is surprisingly insensitive to the many assumptions needed to measure social welfare. Even per capita income exhibited sustained growth between 1947 and 1995, although the rate of growth in the second half of the sample period was much lower. Only median family income is consistent with the claim that living standards are in jeopardy, and for the reasons just described, this index is clearly an inappropriate measure of social welfare.

Inequality in Household Welfare

Income distributional data for families are also frequently used to measure inequality. On the basis of these data, the general view is that inequality has gotten much worse in the United States since the late 1960s. The Gini coefficient of family income, published by the Bureau of the Census, declined gradually from 0.376 in 1947 to 0.348 in 1968. Since then, income inequality increased sharply, attaining a postwar high of 0.430 in 1998.

There are several reasons to expect these inequality estimates to be misleading. If households smooth consumption over time, the distribution of income is likely to be quite different from the expenditure distribution. To the extent that the distributions of tax liabilities and savings change, I would expect the temporal pattern of movements in the distributions of expenditure and income to differ as well. A second problem with using family income to measure inequality arises from the fact that there are no adjustments for differences in the consumption requirements of heterogeneous families. The use of family income to measure welfare requires the assumption that a family of ten is as well off as a family of four if their incomes are the same. The distributional effects of relative price changes are ignored, and perhaps most important, unrelated individuals are excluded from these particular inequality calculations.[20] I consider the importance of each of these potential sources of bias.

The Income and Expenditure Distributions. I initially compare the income and expenditure distributions. Only the *Consumer Expenditure Surveys* (CEX), published by the Bureau of Labor Statistics, provide information on both the incomes and expenditures of the population. These surveys are representative samples of the United States covering the years 1961, 1972, 1973, and 1980 through 1995. The basic observation is a *consumer unit,* which is either a single individual or a group of persons who make joint financial decisions.[21] In each survey, there is comprehensive data on the demographic characteristics of the consumer unit as well as its spending on hundreds of goods and services.[22] There is also detailed information on the levels and sources of income.

I initially compare the raw (unadjusted) distributions of household income and expenditure in each year by tabulating the shares of aggregate income and expenditure going to each decile.[23] In tables 2 and 3, I also present the cumulative shares held by increasing fractions of the population (ranked from the poorest to the richest) as well as the average household sizes for each decile. Comparisons of the cumulative shares show that, relative to the expenditure distribution, the income distribution is more dispersed in each year. In fact, the Lorenz curve of the expenditure distribution lies everywhere inside that of the income distribution, which implies that no matter what index is used to measure inequality, we will find less inequality in the distribution of total expenditure. Note also that average household size increases with the level of income and expenditure, which points to the importance of

TABLE 2
HOUSEHOLD EXPENDITURE DISTRIBUTION, 1961–1995

Share of Aggregate Expenditure by Decile

Year	1	2	3	4	5	6	7	8	9	10
1961	0.026	0.045	0.059	0.072	0.084	0.097	0.112	0.129	0.153	0.221
1973	0.027	0.046	0.060	0.072	0.084	0.097	0.111	0.129	0.153	0.222
1980	0.024	0.044	0.058	0.070	0.083	0.097	0.111	0.129	0.157	0.226
1985	0.024	0.043	0.056	0.069	0.081	0.093	0.108	0.127	0.158	0.242
1990	0.026	0.044	0.057	0.068	0.079	0.092	0.107	0.126	0.156	0.244
1995	0.028	0.047	0.059	0.070	0.081	0.094	0.108	0.127	0.153	0.235

Cumulative Share of Aggregate Expenditure

Year	Bottom 10%	Bottom 20%	Bottom 30%	Bottom 40%	Bottom 50%	Bottom 60%	Bottom 70%	Bottom 80%	Bottom 90%	100%
1961	0.026	0.071	0.131	0.203	0.287	0.385	0.497	0.626	0.779	1.000
1973	0.027	0.073	0.133	0.204	0.288	0.385	0.496	0.625	0.778	1.000

	1	2	3	4	5	6	7	8	9	10
1980	0.024	0.068	0.126	0.196	0.279	0.376	0.488	0.617	0.774	1.000
1985	0.024	0.067	0.122	0.191	0.271	0.365	0.473	0.600	0.758	1.000
1990	0.026	0.071	0.128	0.195	0.274	0.366	0.473	0.599	0.755	1.000
1995	0.028	0.074	0.133	0.203	0.284	0.378	0.485	0.612	0.765	1.000

Average Household Size by Decile

Year	1	2	3	4	5	6	7	8	9	10
1961	1.8	2.3	2.7	3.0	3.3	3.6	3.6	3.8	4.1	4.2
1973	1.5	2.0	2.2	2.5	2.9	3.3	3.4	3.7	3.9	4.2
1980	1.4	1.9	2.3	2.4	2.8	3.2	3.0	3.3	3.5	3.7
1985	1.5	2.0	2.1	2.3	2.6	2.7	2.9	3.2	3.2	3.3
1990	1.6	1.9	2.1	2.3	2.5	2.6	2.9	3.0	3.2	3.3
1995	1.5	1.9	2.1	2.5	2.6	2.6	2.9	3.1	3.0	3.4

SOURCE: Author's calculations from the *Consumer Expenditure Surveys*. Rows in the first panel may not sum to 1 because of rounding.

TABLE 3
HOUSEHOLD INCOME DISTRIBUTION, 1961–1995

Share of Aggregate Income by Decile

Year	1	2	3	4	5	6	7	8	9	10
1961	0.016	0.034	0.051	0.067	0.081	0.095	0.111	0.130	0.157	0.256
1973	0.012	0.030	0.045	0.061	0.077	0.094	0.112	0.133	0.163	0.272
1980	0.011	0.027	0.042	0.058	0.075	0.096	0.116	0.139	0.173	0.264
1985	0.009	0.024	0.036	0.051	0.067	0.087	0.110	0.138	0.181	0.296
1990	0.012	0.026	0.038	0.052	0.069	0.087	0.109	0.138	0.177	0.291
1995	0.010	0.025	0.038	0.052	0.069	0.090	0.112	0.140	0.182	0.283

Cumulative Share of Aggregate Income

Year	Bottom 10%	Bottom 20%	Bottom 30%	Bottom 40%	Bottom 50%	Bottom 60%	Bottom 70%	Bottom 80%	Bottom 90%	100%
1961	0.016	0.051	0.101	0.168	0.250	0.345	0.456	0.587	0.744	1.000
1973	0.012	0.042	0.087	0.148	0.225	0.320	0.432	0.565	0.728	1.000

Year	1	2	3	4	5	6	7	8	9	10
1980	0.011	0.037	0.079	0.137	0.213	0.308	0.424	0.563	0.736	1.000
1985	0.009	0.033	0.070	0.120	0.188	0.275	0.385	0.522	0.704	1.000
1990	0.012	0.038	0.076	0.128	0.198	0.285	0.394	0.532	0.709	1.000
1995	0.010	0.034	0.072	0.124	0.193	0.282	0.394	0.535	0.717	1.000

Average Household Size by Decile

Year	1	2	3	4	5	6	7	8	9	10
1961	1.8	2.5	2.9	3.2	3.3	3.6	3.7	3.7	3.8	3.8
1973	1.5	2.1	2.4	2.7	2.9	3.2	3.4	3.6	3.7	3.8
1980	1.5	2.0	2.1	2.6	2.8	2.9	3.2	3.4	3.4	3.5
1985	2.0	1.9	2.3	2.4	2.4	2.7	2.8	2.9	3.3	3.2
1990	1.6	2.0	2.1	2.3	2.5	2.5	2.8	3.0	3.2	3.2
1995	1.9	1.8	2.2	2.3	2.3	2.8	2.8	3.0	3.1	3.1

SOURCE: Author's calculations from the *Consumer Expenditure Surveys* over the sample of complete income reporters. Rows in the first panel may not sum to 1 because of rounding.

accounting for differences in the consumption requirements of households in measuring inequality.

The shares going to each decile (the first panel in each table) show that the differences between the income and expenditure distributions were pronounced in the upper and lower tails. The bottom 20 percent of the income distribution (the sum of the first two columns) accounted for only 5.1 percent of all income in 1961 and 3.4 percent in 1995. This compares with 7.1 percent and 7.4 percent for the expenditure distribution. The top 20 percent of the income distribution owned 41.3 percent of the total in 1961 and 46.5 percent in 1995; the corresponding shares of the expenditure distribution were 37.4 percent and 38.8 percent.

As important, tables 2 and 3 show that there was more movement in the income distribution over the thirty-five years and, consistent with the findings of other studies, income exhibited increasing dispersion over time.[24] The fraction of aggregate income going to the poorest 50 percent of the population fell sharply from 25.0 percent of the total in 1961 to 19.3 percent in 1995. The expenditure distribution showed much less change, decreasing from 28.7 percent in 1961 to 28.4 percent in 1995. Of course, these tabulations may mask countervailing movements in the upper and lower tails of the distributions.

To measure these types of changes, I report the ratio of the income (and expenditure) share of the top 30 percent to the share going to the bottom 30 percent in table 4. This ratio increased quite dramatically for the income distribution, rising from 5.4 in 1961 to 8.4 in 1995. The corresponding levels for the expenditure distribution were 3.9 in 1961 and 3.9 in 1995. The conclusion is that, in general, there was significant deterioration of the income distribution that was not found with the expenditure distribution.

What accounts for these differences in both the

TABLE 4
RATIO OF THE TOP 30 PERCENT TO THE BOTTOM
30 PERCENT, 1961–1995

Year	Income	Expenditure
1961	5.4	3.9
1973	6.5	3.8
1980	7.3	4.1
1985	8.8	4.3
1990	8.0	4.1
1995	8.4	3.9

SOURCE: Author's calculations from the *Consumer Expenditure Surveys.*

levels of inequality and movements of the distributions? A household's expenditure is the level of before-tax income (including cash transfers) less its tax liabilities, less savings, plus the services from owner-occupied housing and consumer durables. A full explanation of the divergence between the income and expenditure distributions requires an analysis of the distribution of each of these components. The relative importance of each can be assessed by comparing inequality in the distributions of after-tax income and disposable income, where the latter variable is defined to be after-tax income plus the services received from owner-occupied housing and consumer durables.[25]

Inequality indexes for the alternative definitions of income are presented in figure 4. Consistent with the tabulations reported in table 3, before-tax income inequality rose over the sample period, increasing from a level of 0.45 in 1961 to 0.55 by 1995.[26] In 1961 the payment of federal, state, and local taxes reduced inequality from 0.45 to 0.42, implying modest progressivity of the tax system. Between 1961 and 1995, differences between the before- and after-tax income distributions decreased until there was little difference in inequality.

FIGURE 4
INCOME VERSUS EXPENDITURE INEQUALITY, 1961–1995

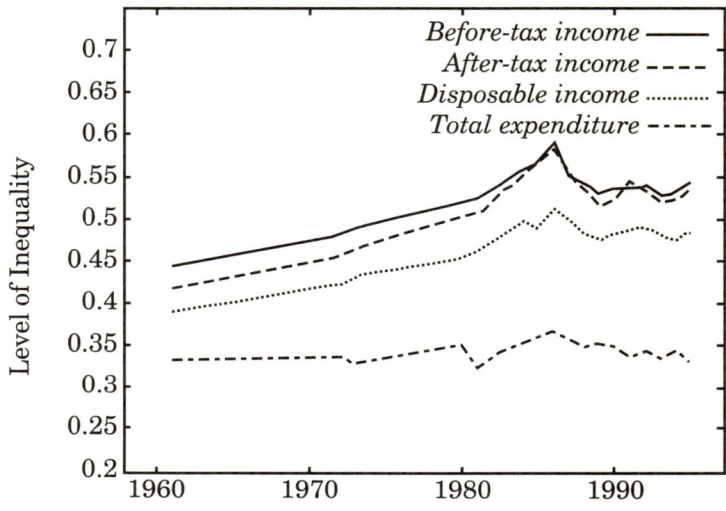

SOURCE: Author's calculations from the *Consumer Expenditure Surveys*. Income inequality indexes are computed for complete income reporters only.

The upward trend in income inequality not only is preserved using after-tax income, but shows an even sharper increase. The differential tax liabilities over this period cannot explain the divergence between the income and expenditure distributions.

Adding the services from durables and owner-occupied housing to after-tax income has an equilibrating effect on the distribution. In 1961 disposable income inequality was 0.39, compared with 0.42 for after-tax income. Inequality in the distribution of total expenditure was 0.33; approximately half of the difference between before-tax income and total expenditure inequality can be explained by taxes and the service flows from durables and housing. The remainder is attributable to the distribution of saving and dissaving.[27]

The service flows from durables and housing remained inequality-reducing in 1995 but accounted for a smaller fraction of the difference between the before-tax income and expenditure distributions. Before-tax income inequality was 0.55, after-tax income inequality was 0.54, disposable income inequality was 0.49, and total expenditure inequality was 0.33.

The divergence between the expenditure and disposable-income distributions was the most important component of the wedge between the before-tax income and expenditure distributions. Although we cannot overlook the possibility that measurement error influenced these distributions, it appears that consumption smoothing and the manner in which it changed between 1961 and 1995 were most influential in explaining the differences between the levels and trends of the income and expenditure inequality indexes. Although an examination of the movements in the distribution of saving and dissaving is beyond the scope of this study, we know that saving is a function of the level and distribution of wealth (human and nonhuman), as well as the changes in the demographic composition of the population (such as age and family size). Both of these determinants of saving changed significantly over this thirty-five-year period.

Household Composition. While the relationship between the income and expenditure distributions is of independent interest, of primary concern is inequality in the distribution of household welfare. A measure of well-being depends not only on the level of total expenditure but also on prices, and on the consumption requirements of households. The importance of accounting for differences in needs is obvious given the systematic variation in average household sizes across deciles. A common misperception is that households with the lowest income or expenditure have the largest families. The CEX data show the opposite correlation;

household size is positively related to the level of expenditure (see table 2). Any correction for needs, therefore, induces a reordering of welfare levels because households with low per equivalent expenditure are different from those that have low levels of (unadjusted) total expenditure.

Per capita expenditure is one of several possible measures of household welfare in which the consumption requirements of households are measured by the number of members. To assess the degree of inequality, I present the deciles of the distribution of per capita expenditure in table 5.[28] Several features of this distribution are particularly noteworthy. Average household size now decreases with the level of per capita expenditure, which confirms the reordering of welfare levels once differences in needs are accounted for. It also shows that failure to account for household heterogeneity gives a distorted picture of which households are poor and which are well-off.

The per capita expenditure distribution is more unequally distributed (except in 1972 and 1973) relative to the household expenditure distribution, but it shows unequivocally less inequality when compared with the household income distribution. In fact, the cumulative shares of the per capita distribution show that its Lorenz curve lies everywhere inside that of the household income distribution. The per capita expenditure distribution also shows somewhat greater deterioration over time relative to the household expenditure distribution, but substantially less than the household income distribution. The fraction of aggregate expenditure going to the bottom 50 percent of the per capita distribution fell from 28.0 percent in 1961 to 26.2 percent in 1995. This compares with a decrease from 25.0 percent to 19.3 percent for household income. The movements in the tails of the distribution are generally consistent with this conclusion. The ratio of the expenditure going to the top 30 percent of the distribution to that going to the bottom 30 percent (table 6) shows that the per capita expenditure distribution deteriorated more than did the distribution of household expenditure, but much less than did the corresponding income distribution. For per capita expenditure, the ratio increased from 4.0 in 1961 to 4.5 in 1995, compared with 5.4 to 8.4 for the income distribution.

The per capita adjustment is one of many possible methods of accounting for differences in the consumption requirements of households. In figure 5, I present inequality indexes for four consumption-based welfare measures that differ only in terms of the equivalence scales used to measure household welfare. In particular, I calculate the level of inequality using equivalence scales that exhibit different economies of scale in consumption. Coulter, Cowell, and Jenkins (1992) have shown that there is a systematic relationship between the degree of economies of scale in consumption and the measured level of inequality. They show that, with a positive correlation between household size and total expenditure, accounting for differences in household size with large economies of scale initially narrows the distribution and lowers the level of inequality. As economies of scale decrease beyond some point, there is a reordering of welfare levels to such an extent that inequality rises.[29]

Estimates that make no adjustment for needs are based on the assumption that the welfare of a household of four is the same as the welfare of a single adult who has the same expenditure. The per capita adjustment is at the opposite extreme and assumes no economies of scale in consumption. The Bureau of the Census scales and the full budget scales are intermediate between these two estimates, with the former assuming substantially greater scale economies.[30]

Figure 5 shows the variation of the inequality estimates that results from employing different equivalence scales. The index calculated using the full budget

TABLE 5
Per Capita Expenditure Distribution, 1961–1995

Share of Aggregate Expenditure by Decile

Year	1	2	3	4	5	6	7	8	9	10
1961	0.026	0.045	0.058	0.069	0.081	0.093	0.108	0.126	0.154	0.239
1973	0.030	0.048	0.059	0.070	0.081	0.093	0.106	0.123	0.152	0.238
1980	0.026	0.043	0.056	0.068	0.079	0.092	0.107	0.127	0.156	0.244
1985	0.024	0.042	0.055	0.066	0.078	0.091	0.106	0.126	0.157	0.254
1990	0.026	0.041	0.052	0.064	0.077	0.090	0.104	0.124	0.156	0.266
1995	0.027	0.042	0.053	0.065	0.076	0.090	0.106	0.128	0.159	0.255

Cumulative Share of Aggregate Expenditure

Year	Bottom 10%	Bottom 20%	Bottom 30%	Bottom 40%	Bottom 50%	Bottom 60%	Bottom 70%	Bottom 80%	Bottom 90%	100%
1961	0.026	0.071	0.129	0.198	0.280	0.373	0.480	0.607	0.761	1.000
1973	0.030	0.077	0.137	0.207	0.288	0.381	0.487	0.610	0.762	1.000

Year	1	2	3	4	5	6	7	8	9	10
1980	0.026	0.070	0.125	0.194	0.273	0.365	0.472	0.599	0.755	1.000
1985	0.024	0.066	0.121	0.187	0.265	0.356	0.462	0.588	0.745	1.000
1990	0.026	0.067	0.119	0.183	0.259	0.350	0.454	0.578	0.734	1.000
1995	0.027	0.068	0.121	0.186	0.262	0.352	0.459	0.586	0.745	1.000

Average Household Size by Decile

Year	1	2	3	4	5	6	7	8	9	10
1961	5.7	4.4	4.1	3.8	3.5	3.3	3.0	2.8	2.4	2.0
1973	5.0	4.2	3.8	3.5	3.3	3.1	2.8	2.6	2.2	1.8
1980	4.5	3.8	3.5	3.3	3.1	2.9	2.6	2.4	2.0	1.7
1985	4.1	3.4	3.1	3.1	2.9	2.6	2.4	2.1	2.1	1.6
1990	4.1	3.7	3.6	3.0	2.7	2.5	2.4	2.2	1.9	1.6
1995	4.4	3.8	3.3	3.1	2.8	2.6	2.4	2.1	1.9	1.5

SOURCE: Author's calculations from the *Consumer Expenditure Surveys*. Rows in the first panel may not sum to 1 because of rounding.

TABLE 6
RATIO OF THE TOP 30 PERCENT TO THE BOTTOM 30 PERCENT, 1961–1995

Year	Household Income	Household Expenditure	Per Capita Expenditure
1961	5.4	3.9	4.0
1973	6.5	3.8	3.7
1980	7.3	4.1	4.2
1985	8.8	4.3	4.4
1990	8.0	4.1	4.6
1995	8.4	3.9	4.5

SOURCE: Author's calculations from the *Consumer Expenditure Surveys*.

FIGURE 5
INEQUALITY IN PER EQUIVALENT CONSUMPTION, 1961–1995

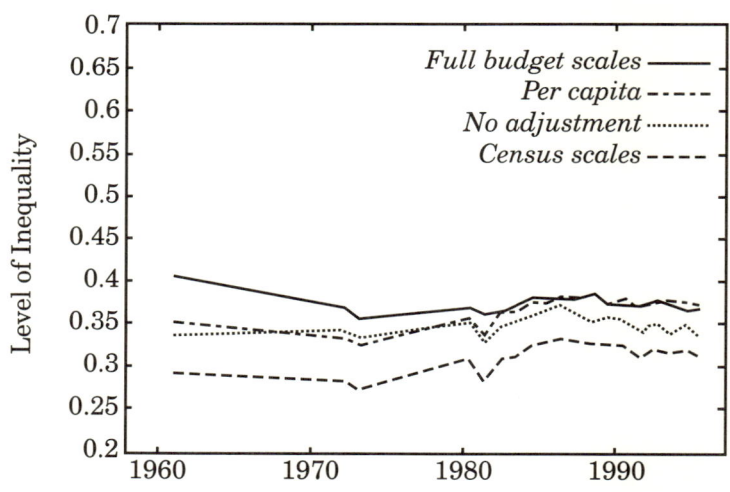

SOURCE: Author's calculations from the *Consumer Expenditure Surveys*. The indexes used to quantify inequality are described by Slesnick (forthcoming).

scales initially decreased between 1961 and 1973 but has not changed much since then. The other estimates of inequality did not change appreciably over the sample period. Inequality in per capita expenditure, for example, was 0.35 in 1961, 0.32 in 1973, 0.35 in 1980, 0.38 in 1990, and 0.37 in 1995. The estimates based on the Bureau of the Census equivalence scales show similar stability ranging from 0.29 in 1961 to 0.31 in 1995.

No matter how I account for differences in needs, the overall conclusion is that the consumption-based inequality measures do not show the sharp deterioration in the distribution that is found when family or household income is used to measure inequality. The inequality measure based on per equivalent consumption (using the full budget scales) shows a decline in inequality through the early 1970s and little change thereafter. The other consumption-based welfare measures show little net change in inequality since 1961.

Distributional Effects of Prices. We know that changes in prices *could* have a potentially large effect on the distribution of well-being if the relative prices of necessities increase. Inflation is often referred to as the "cruelest tax" because of its presumed reduction in the relative purchasing power of the poor compared with the rich. In fact, I find that the effects of changes in relative prices had little effect on the distribution of welfare.

To quantify the distributional effects of price changes, I measure inequality for welfare functions (per equivalent expenditure) with and without household-specific price indexes. These price indexes vary over different types of households to the extent that their spending patterns differ. If the price of food increases sharply, for example, poor households that devote a large fraction of their budgets to food experience a larger increase in the cost of living. Welfare decreases more for them and, as a result, inequality rises. Differences between the inequality indexes shown in figure 6 are exclusively the result of the differential effect of price movements on well-being. It is apparent that prices have had little distributional effect and no influence on the trend in inequality since 1961. This is true even in periods of large changes in relative prices, such as 1973 or the early 1980s. Far from being the cruelest tax, price changes have had almost no (net) distributional impact and certainly cannot explain the divergence between the distributions of per equivalent consumption and family income.[31]

Poverty in the United States

The official poverty rate reported by the Bureau of the Census is based on a definition of absolute poverty de-

FIGURE 6

INEQUALITY IN HOUSEHOLD WELFARE, 1961–1995

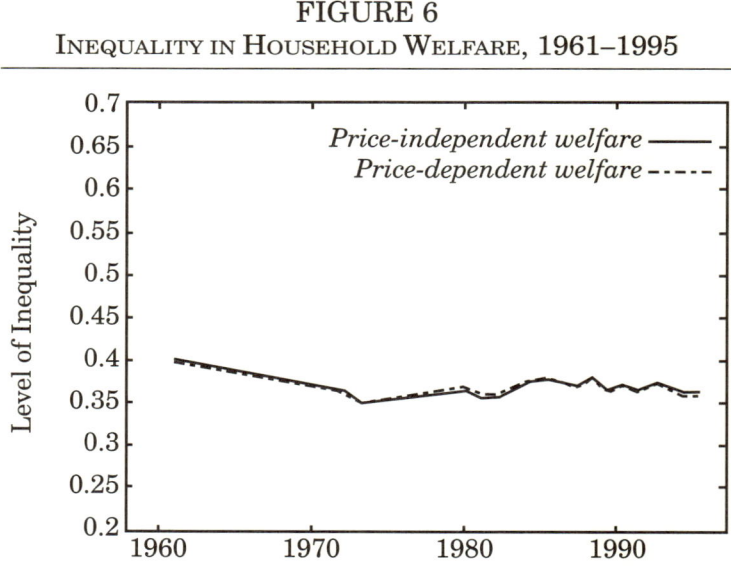

SOURCE: Author's calculations from the *Consumer Expenditure Surveys*. The price-independent index is based on per equivalent expenditure (using full budget scales). The price-dependent index is based on per equivalent expenditure deflated by a household-specific price index, as in equation (1).

veloped in the mid-1960s by the Social Security Administration.[32] At the foundation was an estimate of the subsistence level of food consumption, called the Economy Food Plan (EFP), which was estimated for households distinguished by size, age, gender, and farm or nonfarm residence. For a male-headed, nonfarm family of four, the EFP was approximately $1,000 in 1964. Under the assumption that food represented one-third of all spending by poor households, the poverty line was taken to be three times the amount spent on the EFP.[33]

As prices rise, the costs of purchasing the subsistence market baskets increase. Unless the nominal poverty lines are adjusted upward, they represent the expenditures for lower and lower levels of well-being. To ensure that the thresholds represent a constant standard of living, the poverty lines are adjusted over time using the CPI. Prior to 1969 the thresholds were adjusted on the basis of changes in the cost of food, rather than the CPI itself.

When the Bureau of the Census first began estimating the official poverty rate in the mid-1960s, the only available annual data were income levels reported in the *Current Population Surveys*. Out of practical necessity, households' incomes were used as proxies for consumption. In terms of the welfare function W_k, the official poverty rate was calculated as follows. All members of a household were identified as poor if $W_k < W_z$ where W_z is the poverty line and

$$W_k = \frac{Y_k}{\Pi m_f(A_k)} \qquad (3)$$

and Y_k is the household's before-tax income, A_k is the vector of attributes, $m_f(A_k)$ represents the equivalence scales of the Bureau of the Census, based on households' nutritional requirements, and Π is the CPI.[34]

Although reasonable people can differ in their opinion as to what constitutes a subsistence level of consumption, the conceptual basis of the poverty index developed by the Social Security Administration was quite reasonable. The subsequent implementation by the Census Bureau, however, was plagued by several problems. Household welfare was evaluated using before-tax income, even though poverty was defined using the concept of a subsistence level of consumption. The needs of households were represented by nutritional equivalence scales, which did not reflect the consumption requirements of other items such as housing, utilities, and so on. The bias in the CPI resulted in the overinflation of the poverty lines, particularly in the late 1970s and early 1980s, and the poverty rate was overstated.

The availability of annual expenditure data in the CEX obviates the need to use income as a proxy for consumption in the measurement of poverty. What is the impact of substituting consumption for income in tabulating the poverty rate? To answer this question, I calculate the poverty rate using the welfare function (equation [3]) after substituting total expenditure for income. Differences between this index and the official poverty rate are largely attributable to the substitution of consumption for income in the measurement of the standard of living.[35] To measure the effect of the CPI bias on the poverty rate, a second poverty estimate is tabulated using household expenditures, the same equivalence scales, and the PCE price index.

Figure 7 shows that the poverty rates tabulated using households' expenditures were lower than the official estimates throughout the postwar period, and in most years the differences were very large. In 1961, for example, the poverty rate tabulated using total expenditure was 9.6 percent, compared with the bureau's estimate of 21.9 percent. This gap persisted over the intervening years, and by 1995 the official poverty rate was 13.8 percent, compared with 9.1 percent using expenditures to measure poverty. While the poverty rates tabulated using expenditures were lower than comparable income-based estimates, the trends of the two indexes were similar.

FIGURE 7
INCOME VERSUS CONSUMPTION POVERTY, 1961–1995

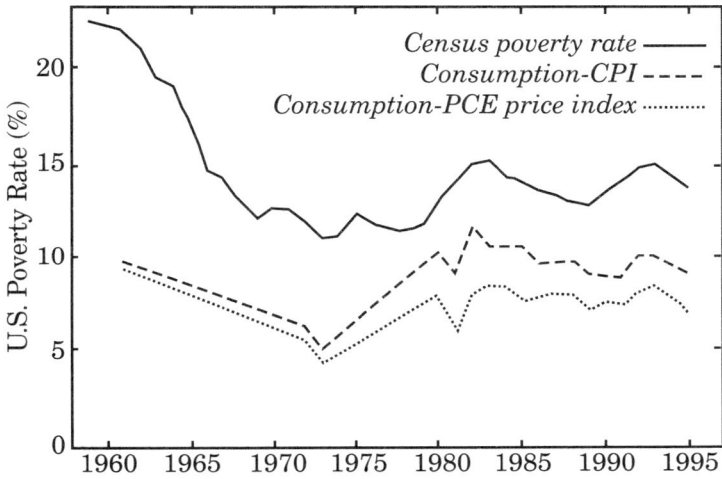

SOURCES: The income-based poverty rate is obtained from the Bureau of the Census. The consumption-based poverty rate is based on the author's calculations from the *Consumer Expenditure Surveys*.

The differences between the two consumption-based indexes in figure 7 illustrate the biases that arise from inflating the poverty lines over time using the CPI. The differences were small until the early 1970s, when the two indexes began to diverge. In 1973 the poverty rate computed using the CPI was 5.0 percent compared with 4.3 percent using the PCE index, but by 1982 the gap widened to 11.6 percent and 7.9 percent. More important, in virtually every year the consumption-based poverty rate computed using an accurate price index was approximately one-half the income-based estimate reported by the Bureau of the Census. By 1995 the official poverty rate was 13.8 percent, compared with 7.0 percent obtained using expenditures and the PCE price index.[36]

The extent of poverty in the United States has been overstated, and figure 7 shows that, by far, the largest source of the bias in the Census Bureau's estimates can be attributed to the use of income as a welfare measure. Why might this be the case? If consumption decisions are based on permanent income, and current income is the sum of the permanent and transitory components, the households with low incomes will have high ratios of consumption to income. Since household welfare depends on the level of consumption, a fixed absolute poverty threshold becomes a smaller and smaller fraction of the overall level of well-being as the average standard of living rises. The income poor will, therefore, have increasing consumption-to-income ratios over time, and current income will deteriorate as a proxy for total expenditure.

Tabulations from the CEX show that a substantial number of individuals are misclassified as poor when income is used to measure poverty. In fact, of all the individuals who are "income poor," a minority are also identified as poor based on their consumption levels. Of the income poor, 59 percent were also consumption poor in 1961, 44 percent in 1973, 42 percent in 1980, 39 percent in 1990, and 33 percent in 1995. This supports the notion that some households are income poor because income is transitorily low, either because they are at the beginning or end of the life cycle or because of random fluctuations in income. Of the households that are income poor but not consumption poor (that is, those who are misclassified as poor), 49 percent in 1961 had a head of household who was either over sixty-five or under twenty-five. In 1973 these households accounted for 50 percent of those misclassified, 55 percent in 1980, 45 percent in 1990, and 36 percent in 1995.[37]

There is ancillary evidence, presented in table 7, that shows that consumption-based welfare estimates more accurately identify the poor. Engel's Law is the empirical observation of an inverse relationship between the food share of total spending and the standard of living. The consumption poor had substantially

TABLE 7
CHARACTERISTICS OF THE POOR

	Consumption Poor			Income Poor		
Year	Food Share (percent)	Home Ownership (percent)	> High School Education (percent)	Food Share (percent)	Home Ownership (percent)	> High School Education (percent)
1961	36.5	16.8	2.3	28.1	41.1	5.3
1973	32.8	18.9	5.5	27.4	39.9	9.4
1980	37.0	15.0	24.6	28.0	39.2	26.0
1985	32.2	21.0	22.2	22.2	43.5	31.1
1990	32.6	12.8	26.0	25.0	35.0	30.0
1995	31.8	13.8	25.3	22.6	35.6	33.9

SOURCE: Tabulations over complete income reporters in the *Consumer Expenditure Surveys*. The educational attainment refers to the head of the household.

higher budget shares of food, compared with the income poor. In 1961, for example, the average food share was 36.5 percent for the consumption poor, compared with 28.1 percent for those classified as poor on the basis of their income. By 1995, food represented 31.8 percent of total spending by the consumption poor and 22.6 percent for the income poor. The latter estimate was not very different from the average share of the entire population.

The frequency of home ownership is also revealing. While roughly 60 percent of all households in the United States lived in their own homes, 16.8 percent of the consumption poor were homeowners in 1961, and the proportion fell to 13.8 percent in 1995. Home ownership among the income poor was much higher throughout the sample period; 41 percent owned homes in 1961, 40 percent in 1973, 39 percent in 1980, and 36 percent in 1995. Perhaps the best indicator of permanent income was the level of educational attainment of the two populations. Consistent with the findings reported above, education levels of the income poor were higher than were those of the consumption poor. The fraction of the heads of households among the consumption poor who had more than a high school education was 2.3 percent in 1961, 5.5 percent in 1973, 24.6 percent in 1980, 26.0 percent in 1990, and 25.3 percent in 1995. The representation among the income poor was significantly higher: 5.3 percent in 1961, 9.4 percent in 1973, 26.0 percent in 1980, 30.0 percent in 1990, and 33.9 percent in 1995.

Conclusions

There is little doubt that family income is the most commonly used indicator of living standards and their distribution in the United States. The Bureau of the Census reports estimates of real median family income and it tabulates poverty rates every year using income as a welfare measure. Inequality is measured using the Gini coefficient of family income. The income-based statistics paint a bleak picture of living standards in the postwar United States.

Although it is widely used, there is little basis in economic theory for using income as a measure of welfare. As a snapshot estimate of the standard of living, the consumption of goods and services is of paramount importance. The standard theoretical paradigm of consumer behavior describes households as constrained utility maximizers, which implies that, for the measurement of welfare, the relevant summary variable is total expenditure rather than income. Income is also unlikely to serve as a reasonable proxy for lifetime income. The existing theories describing the intertemporal allocation of consumption suggest that, with transitory fluctuations in income, households maintain consumption levels either by borrowing (or dissaving) or by saving. As a result, consumption provides a more accurate indicator of intertemporal well-being.

The substitution of income for consumption is an important source of bias in the measurement of living standards, but there are other problems with using family income as an indicator of well-being. Families vary dramatically in terms of their size and composition. To treat all families identically is to assume that different-sized families with the same income are equally well-off. Moreover, restricting consideration to families ignores "unrelated individuals," who currently make up roughly one-third of the total population of families and unrelated individuals; omitting this segment of the population could significantly distort conclusions. Finally, intertemporal comparisons of the standard of living require adjustments for price changes. The CPI is universally used for this purpose, in spite of increasing evidence of systematic upward biases in the estimated inflation rate. This implies, of course, that growth rates of indexes of individual and social welfare are biased downward.

The results presented in this study provide a distinctly different perspective on the evolution of living standards and their distribution in the United States. Using established principles of welfare economics and alternative, consumption-based data sources, I find the emerging picture to be much more optimistic relative to the results obtained using family income.

While real (CPI-deflated) median family income increased 2.6 percent per year between 1947 and 1970, there was little change since then; the average annual growth rate between 1947 and 1995 was only 1.4 percent. The consumption-based estimate of the standard of living increased at an average rate of 2.3 percent per year between 1947 and 1970, and unlike median family income, it continued to increase 1.9 percent per year from 1971 through 1995. On the basis of these estimates, there is no evidence of a stagnant standard of living. Nor do the estimates support the prediction that future generations are at risk of attaining standards of living below those of their parents.

The Bureau of the Census reported that family income inequality decreased through the late 1960s and then increased to its highest postwar level in 1998. Inequality in the distribution of per equivalent consumption showed a similar decrease through the early 1970s but has hardly changed since then. There is no obvious U-turn in inequality. This difference can be explained by several factors. The income distribution is much more unequally distributed relative to expenditures, and most of this difference can be explained by consumption smoothing behavior by households. In addition, there is more movement in the distribution of income relative to expenditures over the years. Consistent with the findings of the Census Bureau, I find that the income distribution has become more unequally distributed, while the expenditure distribution, by contrast, has changed very little.

Another important source of the difference between the distributions of family income and per equivalent consumption arises from the fact that the latter measure accounts for variation in household composition. There is a strong positive correlation between household size and the level of total expenditure. This suggests that adjusting expenditures for differences in the consumption requirements of households will have an important effect on the distribution of welfare. While differences between households do, in fact, influence both levels and trends of inequality, the overall conclusion is that inequality in per equivalent consumption either decreased or changed very little since 1961, depending on the equivalence scales used.

As with the standard of living and inequality, the Census Bureau's poverty statistics paint a discouraging picture. The official poverty rate decreased through the mid-1970s and then reversed trend. As recently as 1993, 15.1 percent of the population was classified as poor, which exceeded the poverty rate attained roughly three decades earlier. Naturally, a number of analysts at both ends of the political spectrum have raised questions about the effectiveness of government programs that were designed to eliminate poverty. Relative to the official statistics, the consumption-based poverty estimates show dramatically lower levels of poverty. That suggests that many of the arguments predicated on high and persistent poverty rates in the United States have to be reexamined.

Why do the consumption-based poverty estimates yield such different conclusions? As with inequality measurement, the substitution of consumption for income in the measurement of welfare is particularly important for explaining differences in both the levels and the trends of poverty. In particular, applying the Bureau of the Census methodology but using expenditures instead of income to identify the poor produces a poverty rate of 9.1 percent in 1995 as compared with the official estimate of 13.8 percent. Replacing the CPI with a PCE price deflator lowers the poverty rate even further to 7.0 percent, a level that is roughly one-half the official estimate.

The infrastructure is in place for federal statistical agencies to move from the current practice of using income to measure the standard of living to a more accurate approach founded on the application of consumption-based methods. Although such a shift will be expensive, the costs pale in comparison with the benefits that would accrue from an accurate measurement of the standard of living of households. Indeed, expensive social programs are often launched (or expanded) on the basis of average income levels. Moving to consumption-based social welfare statistics will help to examine the case for new or expanded programs and to more accurately identify those who most need the assistance.

Notes

1. An alternative approach to welfare measurement that includes components other than material well-being has been proposed by Sen (1985, 1987). See Anand and Ravallion (1993) for a review and discussion of applications in the context of development economics.

2. See Slesnick (1998) for a survey of the theoretical foundation of welfare measurement at both the individual and aggregate levels. See, also, chapter 2 in Slesnick (forthcoming) for a more detailed discussion of these issues.

3. The behavioral basis for the allocation of consumption over time was provided by Friedman (1957) and Modigliani and Brumberg (1954). See Deaton (1992) for a survey of recent empirical work on this issue.

4. Household production issues could change this conclusion. Secondary workers in the household may simply have substituted nonmarket labor for market labor, so that leisure, correctly measured, has not changed.

5. See Moulton (1996) for a description of the methods used to calculate the CPI. A panel of experts convened to study the CPI has concluded that the estimate of inflation is biased upward by roughly 1.1 percent per year (Boskin et al. 1997). This is in addition to permanent errors in the price-level estimates that were introduced in the late 1970s and early 1980s. (Note that

the Bureau of Labor Statistics produces more than one consumer price index. Unless otherwise stated, I am referring to the consumer price index for urban households [CPI-U].)

6. This is the "substitution bias," and empirical estimates put it in the range of 0.1–0.2 percent per year. See Braithwait (1980), Manser and McDonald (1988), and Aizcorbe and Jackman (1993). Boskin et al. (1997) estimate the current bias to be on the order of 0.4 percent per year.

7. A more comprehensive discussion of the housing bias in the CPI is presented by Gillingham and Lane (1982).

8. Kosters (1998) points out that more recent changes in the methods of computing the CPI make temporal comparisons of price changes (and, therefore, inflation-adjusted series) quite difficult. In addition to such problems of internal consistency, Boskin et al. (1997) identify a number of conceptual problems beyond those I have already described. They suggest, for example, that BLS's method of accounting for quality changes introduces another significant upward bias in the inflation estimates.

9. This index is referred to as the CPI-U-X1 (CPIX1 for short) and is identical to the CPI-U after 1983.

10. I also replace durable purchases with the services received from the aggregate stocks. The PCE price index is calculated as a Tornqvist index in which the substitution bias is partially eliminated by allowing the weights in the price index to change as prices change. Note, however, that since the implicit price deflators of the PCE use many of the same components as the CPI, the substitution bias remains a problem at lower levels of disaggregation. For more details on the construction of this index, see Jorgenson and Slesnick (1999) and chapter 4 of Slesnick (forthcoming).

11. Some transfers, such as Social Security, are in-

dexed using the consumer price index for urban wage earners and clerical workers (CPI-W). Many of the same problems exist with that index as well. Estimates of the fiscal impacts of the biases of the CPI are summarized by Boskin and Jorgenson (1997) and Duggan et al. (1995).

12. See Nelson (1993) for further elaboration of this point.

13. See Browning (1992) and Lewbel (1997) for surveys of the methods used to estimate household equivalence scales.

14. For a description of the Bureau of the Census's scales implicit in the poverty estimates, see Orshansky (1965).

15. I address the issue of aggregation in more detail elsewhere (Slesnick 1998, forthcoming).

16. In Slesnick (1991), I present an index of the standard of living that depends on both the level and distribution of well-being among households.

17. The estimate of expenditure is obtained from personal consumption expenditures (PCE) in the National Income and Product Accounts, with durable purchases replaced by estimates of the service flows from the aggregate stocks. More details on this adjustment can be found in Slesnick (1992). Expenditure is deflated by a Tornqvist index calculated using the implicit price deflators of the components of the PCE. Population estimates for the United States are obtained from the Bureau of the Census.

18. An unrelated individual is defined as a person fifteen years old or older who is not living with any relatives. Such an individual could be a single-person household, or could live in group quarters, or could live in a household with other families or unrelated individuals.

19. The latter effect could be particularly important because there have been significant changes in living arrangements over time, with a growing proportion

of people not living with other family members. In 1947, for example, unrelated individuals composed 17 percent of all families and unrelated individuals, compared with 36 percent in 1998.

20. As with the standard of living, this omission could seriously bias the inequality calculations because, on average, unrelated individuals had significantly less income than had families.

21. Consumer units correspond most closely to the Bureau of the Census's population of families and unrelated individuals. The correspondence is imperfect because, for example, two unrelated individuals can live together to form a consumer unit. For ease of exposition, I will refer to consumer units as "households," although it is important to recognize that they are definitionally distinct from what the bureau defines as a household: that is, a group of persons occupying a housing unit.

22. Except for food stamps, in-kind transfers are not included. Several adjustments were made to the Bureau of Labor Statistics definition of total expenditure. I exclude gifts and contributions to retirement programs. Investment expenditures on owner-occupied housing were replaced with the estimated rental equivalent of the home. Purchases of durable goods were replaced with estimates of the services received from the inventory of durables. Topcoded expenditure items were replaced with the topcoded value. I present a more detailed description of these data in chapters 3 and 6 in Slesnick (forthcoming).

23. In these and all subsequent tabulations of the income distribution, I restrict the sample to "complete" income reporters. BLS has a set of criteria that are used to classify a consumer unit as a complete income reporter. In some cases, however, this is a misnomer, because the income report is far from complete even though the consumer unit is classified otherwise. Note, also, that topcoded items were replaced with the top-

coded values. For comparisons of the income data in the CEX with those in the *Current Population Surveys,* see Slesnick (1992).

24. Note that the income distribution does not show the U-turn that was found for the Gini index calculated using family income reported in *Current Population Surveys.* It is difficult to compare the income distributions in the CEX with the CPS because the observational units and sample coverage are quite different. That is, a consumer unit is distinct from the bureau's definition of a family (or a household, for that matter). Cutler and Katz (1991), however, report that the per capita distributions of income in the CEX and CPS (which *are* comparable) are similar.

25. After-tax income is before-tax income less the sum of federal, state, and local taxes. The taxes reported by each household in the CEX are the net taxes paid over the previous twelve months. No attempt has been made to assess the accuracy of the reported tax payments. Bosworth, Burtless, and Sabelhaus (1991) claim that the tax reports in the 1972 and 1973 CEX appear to be accurate, while those in the 1980s are unreliable. This would clearly affect the trends of the after-tax and disposable income inequality indexes in figure 4.

26. Inequality is measured using a variant of an Atkinson (1970) index, with household welfare represented by the log of income or expenditure. The index lies between zero and one, with the minimum value attained when every household has the same income or expenditure. This measure of inequality can be interpreted as the proportional loss in social welfare attributable to an unequal distribution of well-being and has virtually all of the commonly used inequality indexes as special cases (Blackorby and Donaldson [1978]). A more detailed description of the specific index used in figure 4 is presented in chapter 6 of Slesnick (forthcoming).

27. Given the nature of the data, this interpreta-

tion must be qualified. The difference between disposable income and total expenditure is also the "dumping ground" of measurement errors associated with each component of disposable income and consumption. The extent to which there are differential errors of measurement at different points of the distribution will distort the estimate of the impact of consumption smoothing on differences between the income and expenditure distributions. That suggests that caution is in order in interpreting the differences as being the result of saving.

28. An equal sharing rule is assumed, so that each individual in a household is assumed to have the same expenditure. The distribution is tabulated over all individuals (rather than households) in the sample. The household size estimates represent the average size of the households of the individuals belonging to each respective decile.

29. That is, large families with above-average household expenditure are in the bottom end of the per capita expenditure distribution. Banks and Johnson (1994) show that this relationship no longer holds once one distinguishes households by characteristics other than the number of persons in the household. If one treats children differently from adults, for example, the relationship between inequality and the economies of scale in consumption no longer holds.

30. The Bureau of the Census equivalence scales and the full budget equivalence scales used in figure 5 also vary over characteristics other than family size. See chapter 5 of Slesnick (forthcoming) for a more complete description of each set of equivalence scales.

31. Newbery (1995) found that price changes had little effect on the distribution of welfare in the United Kingdom and Hungary.

32. An absolute poverty index identifies the poor using a fixed threshold that is usually tied to a subsistence budget. Some analysts have advocated a relative measure of poverty in which the poor are identified on

the basis of how they are doing relative to others. Arguments in favor of the relative approach to poverty measurement are presented by Townsend (1985) and Sen (1983). To operationalize the concept, Fuchs (1967) suggested that the "relative poverty line" be 50 percent of median income.

33. There are other minor modifications to this general method of setting the poverty line for smaller households. See Orshansky (1965) and Ruggles (1990) for a complete description of the U.S. poverty line.

34. These equivalence scales are reported in chapter 5 in Slesnick (forthcoming) and are obtained from the 1964 weighted poverty thresholds reported in Orshansky (1966), table 1, p. 23.

35. There are other minor differences. I use $2,998 as the poverty line for a family of four in 1964 and adjust the threshold using the same equivalence scales and price index (the CPI) throughout the sample period. The official estimates embody a number of changes in the equivalence scales and the price adjustments. See Ruggles (1990) for further discussion.

36. There are reasons to believe that these consumption-based estimates are conservative and that the poverty rates tabulated using expenditures are overstated in the 1980s and 1990s. See chapter 7 in Slesnick (forthcoming) for further discussion.

37. In keeping with expectations, the "permanent income" or "consumption" poor also tend to have low income. In 1961, 83 percent of the consumption poor were also income poor. The overlap was 64 percent in 1973, 59 percent in 1980, 63 percent in 1990, and 61 percent in 1995.

References

Aizcorbe, A. M., and P. C. Jackman. 1993. "The Commodity Substitution Effect in CPI Data." *Monthly Labor Review* 116, no. 12 (December): 25–33.

Anand, S., and M. Ravallion. 1993. "Human Development in Poor Countries: On the Role of Private Incomes and Public Services." *Journal of Economic Perspectives* 7, no. 1 (Winter): 113–50.

Atkinson, A. B. 1970. "On Measurement of Inequality." *Journal of Economic Theory* 2, no. 3 (September): 244–63.

Banks, J., and P. Johnson. 1994. "Equivalence Scale Relativities Revisited." *Economic Journal* 104, no. 425 (July): 883–90.

Blackorby, C., and D. Donaldson. 1978. "Measures of Relative Inequality and Their Meaning in Terms of Social Welfare." *Journal of Economic Theory* 18, no. 1 (June): 651–75.

Boskin, M., and D. Jorgenson. 1997. "Implications of Overstating Inflation for Indexing Government Programs and Understanding Economic Progress." *American Economic Review* 87, no. 2 (May): 89–93.

Boskin, M., E. Dulberger, R. Gordon, Z. Griliches, and D. Jorgenson. 1997. "The CPI Commission: Findings and Recommendations." *American Economic Review* 87, no. 2 (May): 78–83.

Bosworth, B., G. Burtless, and J. Sabelhaus. 1991. "The Decline in Saving: Evidence from Household Surveys." *Brookings Papers on Economic Activity,* no. 1: 183–241.

Braithwait, S. D. 1980. "The Substitution Bias of the Laspeyres Price Index." *American Economic Review* 70: 64–77.

Browning, M. 1992. "Children and Household Economic Behavior." *Journal of Economic Literature* 30, no. 3 (September): 1434–75.

Coulter, F., F. Cowell, and S. Jenkins. 1992. "Equivalence Scale Relativities and the Extent of Inequality and Poverty." *Economic Journal* 102 (September): 1067–82.

Cutler, D., and L. Katz. 1991. "Macroeconomic Performance and the Disadvantaged." *Brookings Papers on Economic Activity,* no. 2: 1–74.

Deaton, A. 1992. *Understanding Consumption.* Oxford: Oxford University Press.

Duggan, J., R. Gillingham, and J. Greenlees. 1995. "Housing Bias in the CPI and Its Effects on the Budget Deficit and the Social Security Trust Fund." Unpublished manuscript.

Friedman, M. 1957. *A Theory of the Consumption Function.* Princeton: Princeton University Press.

Fuchs, V. 1967. "Redefining Poverty and Redistributing Income." *Public Interest* 8 (Summer): 88–95.

Gillingham, R., and W. Lane. 1982. "Changing the Treatment of Shelter Costs for Homeowners in the CPI." *Monthly Labor Review* 105 (June): 9–14.

Jorgenson, D., and D. Slesnick. 1999. "Indexing Government Benefits for Changes in the Cost of Living." *Journal of Business and Economic Statistics* 77, no. 2 (April): 170–81.

Kosters, M. H. 1998. *Wage Levels and Inequality: Measuring and Interpreting the Trends.* Washington, D.C.: AEI Press.

Lewbel, A. 1997. "Consumer Demand Systems and Household Equivalence Scales." *Handbook of Applied Econometrics, vol. II: Microeconomics.* Ed.

M. H. Pesaran and P. Schmidt (Oxford: Blackwell Publishers Ltd.).

Manser, M. E., and R. J. McDonald. 1988. "An Analysis of Substitution Bias in Measuring Inflation, 1959–1985." *Econometrica* 56, no. 4 (July): 909–30.

Modigliani, F., and R. Brumberg. 1954. "Utility Analysis and the Consumption Function: An Interpretation of Cross Section Data." In *Post Keynesian Economics,* ed. K. Kurihara. New Brunswick: Rutgers University Press, pp. 388–436.

Moulton, B. R. 1996. "Bias in the Consumer Price Index: What Is the Evidence?" *Journal of Economic Perspectives* 10, no. 4 (Fall): 159–77.

Nelson, J. A. 1993. "Household Equivalence Scales: Theory versus Policy." *Journal of Labor Economics* 11, no. 3: 471–93.

Newbery, D. M. 1995. "The Distributional Impact of Price Changes in Hungary and the United Kingdom." *Economic Journal* 105, no. 431 (July): 847–63.

Orshansky, M. 1965. "Counting the Poor: Another Look at the Poverty Profile." *Social Security Bulletin* 28, no. 1 (January): 3–29.

———. 1966. "Recounting the Poor—A Five Year Review." *Social Security Bulletin* 29, no. 4 (April): 20–37.

Ruggles, P. 1990. *Drawing the Line: Alternative Poverty Measures and Their Implications for Public Policy.* Washington, D.C.: Urban Institute Press.

Sen, A. K. 1983. "Poor, Relatively Speaking." *Oxford Economic Papers* 35: 153–69.

———. 1985. *Commodities and Capabilities.* Amsterdam: North Holland.

———. 1987. *The Standard of Living.* Cambridge: Cambridge University Press.

Slesnick, D. T. 1991. "The Standard of Living in the United States." *Review of Income and Wealth,* Series 37, no. 4 (December): 363–86.

————. 1992. "Aggregate Consumption and Saving in the Postwar United States." *Review of Economics and Statistics* 74, no. 4 (November): 585–97.

————. 1993. "Gaining Ground: Poverty in the Postwar United States." *Journal of Political Economy* 101, no. 1 (February): 1–38.

————. 1994. "Consumption, Needs and Inequality." *International Economic Review* 35, no. 3 (August): 677–703.

————. 1998. "Empirical Approaches to the Measurement of Welfare." *Journal of Economic Literature* 36, no. 4 (December): 2108–65.

————. Forthcoming. *Consumption and Social Welfare: Living Standards and Their Distribution in the United States.* Cambridge: Cambridge University Press.

Townsend, P. 1985. "A Sociological Approach to the Measurement of Poverty: A Rejoinder to Professor Amartya Sen." *Oxford Economic Papers* 37, no. 4 (December): 659–68.

About the Author

DANIEL T. SLESNICK is the Rex G. Baker, Jr., Professor of Political Economy at the University of Texas at Austin. He has published articles on welfare economics and applied econometrics that have appeared in leading peer-reviewed journals, including the *Journal of Political Economy,* the *Review of Economic Studies,* the *Economic Journal,* and the *Journal of Econometrics.* He is the author of the forthcoming book *Consumption and Social Welfare: Living Standards and Their Distribution in the United States.*

AEI STUDIES ON UNDERSTANDING ECONOMIC INEQUALITY
Marvin H. Kosters, series editor

ATTITUDES TOWARD ECONOMIC INEQUALITY
Everett Carll Ladd and Karlyn H. Bowman

COMPARING POVERTY: THE UNITED STATES AND OTHER INDUSTRIAL NATIONS
McKinley L. Blackburn

THE DISTRIBUTION OF WEALTH: INCREASING INEQUALITY?
John C. Weicher

EARNINGS INEQUALITY: THE INFLUENCE OF CHANGING OPPORTUNITIES AND CHOICES
Robert H. Haveman

INCOME INEQUALITY AND IQ
Charles Murray

INCOME MOBILITY AND THE MIDDLE CLASS
Richard V. Burkhauser, Amy D. Crews, Mary C. Daly, and Stephen P. Jenkins

INCOME REDISTRIBUTION AND THE REALIGNMENT OF AMERICAN POLITICS
Nolan M. McCarty, Keith T. Poole, and Howard Rosenthal

LABOR COSTS AND INTERNATIONAL TRADE
Stephen S. Golub

LIVING STANDARDS IN THE UNITED STATES: A CONSUMPTION-BASED APPROACH
Daniel T. Slesnick

RELATIVE WAGE TRENDS, WOMEN'S WORK, AND FAMILY INCOME
Chinhui Juhn

THE THIRD INDUSTRIAL REVOLUTION: TECHNOLOGY, PRODUCTIVITY, AND INCOME INEQUALITY
Jeremy Greenwood

WAGE INEQUALITY: INTERNATIONAL COMPARISONS OF ITS SOURCES
Francine D. Blau and Lawrence M. Kahn

WAGE LEVELS AND INEQUALITY: MEASURING AND INTERPRETING THE TRENDS
Marvin H. Kosters